ADALENE
plays many ways

To Lowie, for teaching me so much about myself.
May your curious, yet gracious spirit continue
to create more space for others.
And to my A, for literally supporting me with every step.
–Erika

To Noah and Livia
–Karalie

written by

ERIKA JOY SNEATH

ADALENE

plays many ways

illustrated by

KARALIE JURASKA

It was a clear, sunshiny day, and Adalene was so excited she could hardly eat her breakfast. Talking with a mouthful, she leaned in to Grandma and said, "I can't wait to play with Uncle E!"

"It's such a cheery day to go to the park!" Grandma replied.

It was only 8 o'clock in the morning, and Everett was already concerned. Despite very much looking forward to spending time with Adalene, he couldn't help but anticipate the uncertainty of the day.

Adalene spent the morning playing with her animal friends and coloring. After what felt like hours, Dad announced it was time to go. They grabbed their things and were out the door.

As they walked to the park, Adalene counted the neighbors' beautiful sunflowers. "I can't wait to tell Uncle E I saw five sunflowers!" Adalene shared with her dad.

Everett got ready for the day slowly
and took his medication, and pretty soon
it was time to go. He grabbed his keys,
balanced carefully on the railing down
the stairs, and drove off.

"E!" Adalene cried when they got to the park. I'm so glad you're here. Isn't it a wonderful day?"

"It is just beautiful out. And you know how much I love summer!" Everett replied.

"We saw five sunflowers on the walk over, E!" Adalene reached for Everett's hand and gave a tug. "Hey, will you help me on the ladder?" she asked enthusiastically.

Everett scanned the play structure. "Why don't we wait for your dad to finish setting up the picnic, and he can help you?"

"Dad! Can you come over here?" Adalene called to him. She was feeling impatient.

Everett looked a little nervous. Should he have helped her up the ladder?

With her dad's help, Adalene climbed up the ladder, then ran over the bridge, and shouted from the tower, "I'm on top of the wooorld!"

She looked around. "Hey, E, can you come play up here with me?" Adalene loved spending time with her Uncle E.

Everett looked around. "I'd love to!"
he exclaimed.

After climbing up, he crouched down and
peeked through the telescope on the
tower. "Look at those daisies."

Adalene peered through to admire them
too. Everett was relieved he was enjoying
playing with Adalene.

Not long after, Adalene tagged him and
said, "You're it! The ground is lava!"

Adalene hopped through the barrier, bounced on the bongo jungle climber, skipped to the top step, and looked back. Why wasn't Everett trying to catch up to her?

Everett was still standing at the top.
He called out to Adalene that he needed
a break.

Adalene hesitated for a moment, then
slowly started dragging her feet as she
went back to meet him at the picnic table.

"Hey, Adalene, thanks for coming over. I'm pretty disappointed that I'll need to stop and rest for a bit."

"Oh, that's okay; here's a juice box!"

Everett enjoyed the calm moment to sip his juice. Adalene slurped hers quickly to get back to playing.

"Okay, are you ready? Let's go!"
Adalene announced.

"Not yet, but I can rest here while you play on the monkey bars. Why don't you hand me that pillow on your way?"

"Sure, E, let me get this set up for you."

Everett watched Adelene swing from one rung to the next. He wished he could have played more, but he knew it was time to head home. He promised to see Addy later that week.

Everett spent the rest of his day resting
on the couch while Adalene continued
playing. "Why didn't Uncle E want to stay
longer?" She wondered to herself.

That night when Grandma tucked Adalene in, she sensed something was bothering her Addy. "Sweetie, what are you feeling tonight?" Grandma asked with care.

"Well, Grandma, I want to tell you something, but I don't want you to be mad."

"Anytime you are open to sharing your feelings, I'd love to listen," Grandma replied.

"Does Uncle Everett like playing with me? Last weekend he was building blocks, and we were just laughing and having fun. Today he didn't want to play. I'm confused by that, and it makes me sad."

"Thank you for sharing with me. I hear where you're coming from. It must have been really disappointing when he wasn't able to play."

"Yeah," Adalene replied.

"That makes sense. I'm curious, did it seem like he was having fun?"

"Maybe a little bit. It was hard to tell. I really wanted him to play tag with me!"

"I'm wondering if Everett was in more pain this morning at the park." Grandma shared.

"I bet he really wanted to play but decided not to. Sometimes a lot of playing makes him too tired for everything else in the day."

"How can you tell? He was smiling and so excited to see me at the park, Grandma!" Adalene wondered.

"Honestly, sweet Addy, you usually can't tell. There are many people who suffer from chronic pain or illnesses that, according to most, look 'normal.'

I know for a fact that Everett absolutely loves being your uncle. If he had it his way, he would have played tag all day!"

Grandma continued, "It's okay for you to be disappointed. I'm sad too. I used to love it when Everett helped me in my garden. I think about him when I tend to my plants, and I also bring over fresh flowers for his table when I visit.

"When we play cards, we have something pretty to look at. He also offers ideas of what I should plant next and helps me research what steps I need to take for that process.

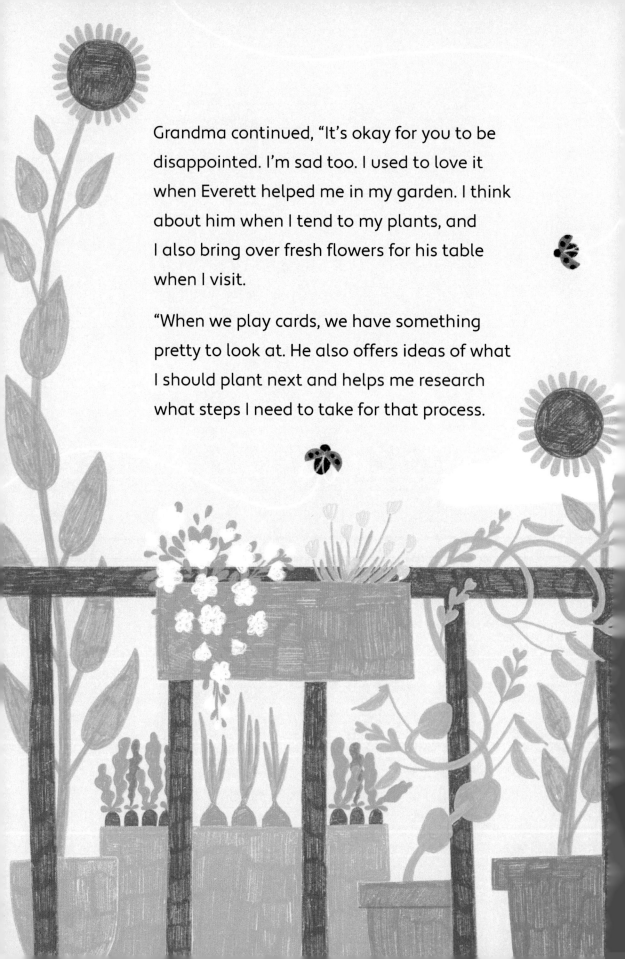

"Thinking of a different activity to do together is one way to demonstrate your care and understanding of his pain. Is there another activity you could do with him another day?"

"Maybe I'll ask him to read a couple of books with me?" Adalene suggested.

"That sounds really nice, Addy. Now sleep tight!"

The next morning, Adalene called her
Uncle Everett. "Uncle E, would it be okay
with you if I came over? I'd love to read
with you!"

"I would absolutely love that, Adalene.
I'll see you soon!"

The End

Erika Joy (TenHaken) Sneath,
M.S., is an experienced educator with specialties in curriculum, reading, English language development, social-emotional learning, and special education.

After navigating multiple ankle injuries and surgeries, she eventually began accepting that chronic pain is a part of her story. Stemming from a place of promoting inclusion, Erika invites others to learn and grow alongside her.

Connect with her further via www.erikajoysneath.com.

Karalie Juraska grew up crafting and creating. These loves led her to pursue an education and career in graphic design. Now, working as a freelance designer and illustrator from her home in Portland, Oregon, Karalie has found her sweet spot collaborating with small businesses, individuals and non-profits. She cares about making simple, beautiful, and thoughtful work.

Karalie is also a wife and mother. She loves spending time in the garden, around the table and over a good picture book with her family.

To connect with Karalie, please visit karaliejuraska.com.

A special thank you to our contributors...

Adelina Rotar, Alina Sayre, Alyssa Choudhry, Angelica Bronson, Anonymous, Audrey Dhillon, Barbara Nichols, Bill and Lorraine TenHaken, Bob and Shirley TenHaken (Grandpa & Grandma), Brian and Becky Gilmore, Cary and Kelsey Samsel, Casey Sinigalia, Cory Greenberg, Cyndie Snyder, Cynthia Becker, Danny Cossey, DJ Ruggiero, Doug Croze, Duane and Liz Larson, Elizabeth Mundt, Ellen Quade, Geena Bergen, Grace Schroeder, Hannah Chan, Hannah Patton, Jalee Lockman, Jan Poujade, Jana Riedel, Jenny Meadow, Jeremy and Natalie Won, Jesse Roselin, Jessica Arnzen, Joan Christensen, Joanna Small, Kathy Tojaga, Katrina and Ashton Dunbar, Keri Jackson, Kimberly Shryer, Kirsten and Josh TenHaken-Riedel, Kristen Burns, Kristin Clayton, Lauren Hollister, Lia Stavoravdi-Stoll, Lois Larson (Mormor), Marion Davis, Mary Bocci-Collins, Mel Nichols, Melodie and Nick Gregg, Michelle Terpstra, Molly Tweten, Randy and Charlene Dalzell, Rebecca & Brandon Winebrenner, Rebecca Klouwers, Renee A Russell, Sarah and Murphy Carroll, Staci Stutsman, Steve and Lisa Tyler, Susan Guenther, Taylor Boe, Taylor Virtue, Tiffany Bachman, Tony and Leanne Sneath, Tracy Guan

Made in the USA
Monee, IL
20 June 2023

35846513R00021